Eating Disorders

Look for these and other books in the Lucent
Overview series:

Eating
Disorders

by Don Nardo

LUCENT
B·O·O·K·S

Library of Congress Cataloging-in-Publication Data

Nardo, Don, 1947-
    Eating disorders / by Don Nardo.
        p.   cm. — (Lucent overview series)
    Includes bibliographical references and index.
    Summary: Examines the nature of eating disorders, their causes,
warning signs, and effects, and how to deal with them.
    ISBN 1-56006-129-4
    1. Eating disorders—Juvenile literature.   2. Eating disorders—
Treatment—Juvenile literature.   [1. Eating disorders.]
I. Title.   II. Series.
RC552.E18N37   1991
616.85'26 — dc20   91-15563

Contents

Introduction

IN 1982, *STARVING for Attention*, a book written by Cherry Boone O'Neill, daughter of singer and actor Pat Boone, became a best-seller. In the book, O'Neill frankly told of her long ordeal with anorexia nervosa and bulimia nervosa, two related and very harmful eating disorders. People with anorexia starve themselves and suffer severe weight loss. Bulimia is a disorder that causes people to periodically binge, or overeat, and then try to eliminate the food they have eaten, usually by vomiting. According to her dramatic account, O'Neill became so obsessed with food that her life began to fall apart. She alternated between starving herself and gorging herself with junk food. Her behavior became so strange that she sometimes ate slimy scraps from a dog's bowl. She ended up in the hospital, weighing only eighty pounds and near death. Eventually, however, she managed to recover from her eating disorders and learned to lead a normal life once again.

O'Neill was the first celebrity to publicly admit that she had such serious eating problems and to describe her painful experiences in such stark detail. The book touched a nerve with readers. She received thousands of letters from young women who said they, too, suffered from anorexia

(opposite page) Popular singer Karen Carpenter's gaunt face betrays her battle with anorexia in this 1981 photo taken at an awards ceremony. Her death two years later was directly related to her eating disorder.

and bulimia. Many had never before heard that there were medical names for their problems. They wrote that they had been miserable for years but had suffered in silence, not knowing there were other people with such problems. Some told how their obsession with food had ruined their health or broken up their marriages. When O'Neill told her story on TV and radio talk shows, the phone lines were always jammed. The callers admitted they had the same harmful eating habits she described and begged for advice on how to overcome them.

After O'Neill's book was published, anorexia and bulimia began to receive more and more public attention. In January 1983, the news media reported that popular singer Karen Carpenter had died of heart failure as a result of prolonged self-starvation. Family members described how she had suffered from anorexia for several years. All attempts by family and friends to help her overcome the disorder had failed. Her tragic death emphasized that eating disorders are more than unhealthy and emotionally disturbing. They can also be fatal. Also in 1983, the well-known actress and exercise advocate Jane Fonda admitted to being bulimic as a teenager and young adult. Other celebrities, such as gymnast Cathy Rigby and actresses Susan Dey and Ally Sheedy, admitted that they had also suffered from eating disorders.

More public attention

These confessions of famous people were important because they focused attention on eating disorders. The stories gave hope to many other sufferers, and made them realize how serious their own eating problems were. This prompted them to seek professional help. Doctors and medical authorities began to understand how widespread these disorders had become. Studies con-

ducted in the late 1980s showed that as many as 10 percent of American women may suffer from one or more eating disorders. Experts estimate that on college campuses, the figure may be as high as 20 percent. Men also suffer from these disorders but in far fewer numbers.

It is safe to say that although they do not realize it, almost everyone knows someone with an eating disorder. Most who suffer from eating disorders do so in secret, afraid or unwilling to discuss their behavior or to seek help. Their family, friends, and coworkers may have no idea they are sick. Because people with these disorders are so unhappy, their relationships, marriages, and jobs often suffer. As a result, eating disorders affect a wide range of people, either directly or indirectly.

Eating disorders afflict many women who are involved in sports like gymnastics and dance. Champion gymnast Cathy Rigby struggled to overcome an eating disorder that threatened her career and her life.

1

Why People Eat

Editor's Note: The people quoted in this book who do not wish their identity revealed are referred to only by their first name or first name and last initial.

PEOPLE WITH EATING disorders are obsessed with food and, in one way or another, abuse it. Unlike people who abuse alcohol and drugs and can overcome their problems by avoiding these substances, food abusers have to eat food in order to survive. People with eating disorders are exposed constantly to the very substance they have a problem with. Since they cannot avoid food, these people must overcome their eating problems by learning to deal with food in a rational, healthy way.

Food's popular image

Most of those suffering from eating disorders find that learning to deal with their food obsession is very difficult. They say that one reason for this is the importance society places on food and eating. There is little doubt that early, primitive human beings ate primarily to survive. But this is no longer the case. As eating disorder specialist Hilde Bruch put it, "There is no human society . . . that eats according to the availability, edibility, and nutritional value [of food] alone." The preparation, presentation, and advertisement of

(opposite page) A banquet guest prepares to indulge his appetite in a virtual sea of food. For humans, food satisfies emotional needs for joy, security, and abundance as well as satisfying physical hunger.

11

food have become important elements in every-one's life. On television, in magazines and news-papers, and at countless social functions, people are constantly encouraged to eat.

Most people are able to deal with the abundance of food and food images without becoming food abusers. For those who do not suffer from eating disorders, food and eating are just another part of life.

By contrast, food abusers regard food as one of the most important aspects of their lives. Joan C., who suffered for twelve years from both bulimia and anorexia, said, "Food was the only thing I ever looked forward to. . . . I was obsessed with food and thought about it day and night." Like other people with eating disorders, Joan felt surrounded by food. Her painful daily battle with eating was made all the more difficult by a culture seemingly as obsessed with food as she was. She wished that eating could be just a simple matter of satisfying her hunger. But she realized that there are too many other reasons and occasions for eating.

Hunger and appetite

Hunger is a basic, physical response to a lack of food. Food is fuel for the body, and everyone must regularly consume that fuel in order to survive. The physical sensation of hunger—usually consisting of uncomfortable feelings in the stomach, restlessness, and sometimes weakness and headache—is the body's way of saying it is low on fuel. A hungry person eats something, and the sensation of hunger temporarily disappears. But if human beings ate only to satisfy their hunger, there would be few fat people and no one would suffer from eating disorders.

As medical historian Joan Jacobs Brumberg commented, "In our society food is chosen and

eaten not merely on the basis of hunger." The fact is that people also eat to satisfy their appetite. Appetite is the desire, or craving, for food, often a specific kind of food. The look, smell, taste, and texture of various foods are factors that influence appetite. In general, hunger is a feeling associated with the physical need for food, while appetite is associated with the enjoyment of food.

Often, eating satisfies both hunger and appetite at the same time. For instance, if a person is hungry and craves pasta, eating a bowl of spaghetti will give the body fuel and quench the desire. But the two feelings do not always go together. If they get hungry enough, for example, many people will eat foods they find extremely unappetizing. On the other hand, some people are attracted to appetizing foods even when they are not hungry. Appetite is mainly an expression of food likes and dislikes, which are shaped by habit and

Busy people eat a fast-food lunch outside their office building. Today, people often sacrifice nutrition for the convenience and taste of fast foods.

past experiences with food. That is why people raised in a certain culture often consider the foods they are used to as the most appetizing and reject unfamiliar foods from other cultures.

Most of the social customs, practices, and commercial advertisements dealing with eating emphasize the appetizing, rather than the nutritional, aspects of food. By appealing to the appetite, popular culture constantly promotes the idea that food is something to be desired. Eating to satisfy appetite, rather than to satisfy hunger, can have significant consequences. Even for the majority of people who do not suffer from eating disorders, the desire for food can lead to overeating, which can affect weight, health, and appearance.

Because of the way society promotes food, those who do suffer from eating disorders find it difficult to deal with their individual eating problems. Everywhere they turn, their culture depicts food as something important, something special, something to look forward to and enjoy. Whether at home, at work, or in public, they are bombarded by images and ideas about food and eating.

Attitudes toward food in the home

It is in the home that most people first interact with food and recognize its importance. Children learn that they cannot get food on their own and must rely on their parents for it. Because a child feels confident that a parent will supply meals on a regular basis, food helps build a feeling of trust between parent and child. The child trusts that the parent will continue supplying food, no matter what happens. The act of giving food becomes an important expression of the parent's love and generosity.

The act of giving food can also be an expression of power. Because a parent can acquire food and the child cannot, the child sees the parent as a

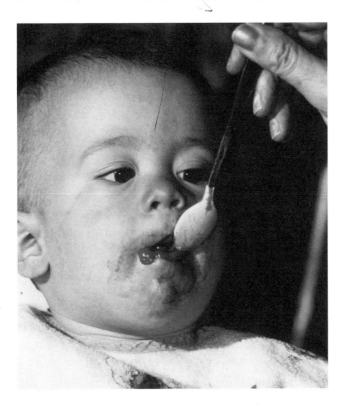

Parents often use food to reward or punish behavior. As adults, many people continue to reward themselves with food.

powerful figure. Some parents use their power over the food supply to persuade their children to behave in a certain way. Food then becomes a tool that can be used either to punish or reward a child. Common food punishments include being sent to bed with no dinner, having to eat last night's dinner cold for breakfast, and missing out on dessert. Often, parents use food as a reward for good behavior by giving children extra desserts, offering to cook their favorite meals, or buying them candy and other treats. In this way, many children and parents come to see food not only as nourishment but also as an important tool in shaping behavior.

In addition, in a majority of households, food is a means for gathering the family together. More communication among family members takes place during meals than at any other time.

Peter Dally, a doctor and expert on eating disorders, has pointed out, "Most meals are sociable occasions; not only is food shared, but news, ideas, plans and feelings. . . . For someone to eat alone habitually, from choice, is unusual, a sign that all is not well."

Many of the social skills children develop are associated with mealtime. As adults, they continue to socialize and communicate around food. "We'll talk about it over dinner," and "Let's have lunch," are common invitations to share information or feelings. And many important business deals are made over food and drink.

Showing off with food

Food is also used to impress others. Often, people try to show how wealthy they are by treating guests to an elaborate meal. Dally says, "A meal may proclaim the prosperity and values of the host." In an effort to impress the guests, the host might prepare expensive or exotic foods or

This gourmet chef is proud of his skill and creativity in making food appear, smell, and taste especially appetizing.

serve the food with costly china and glassware. Or the guests might be "taken to an expensive restaurant where not only the host's wealth but his discriminating [refined] tastes are displayed," according to Dally. In these cases, a meal has very little to do with nutrition and a great deal to do with social status.

The preparation of a home-cooked meal is also a way for the host to show off his or her talents. Many people take pride in their cooking and entertaining abilities. Usually, they are less concerned with how nourishing the food is than with how good it looks, smells, and tastes and with how nice the house appears. They are thrilled when a guest asks for seconds, proof that the meal is a hit. If a guest only nibbles at the food or politely refuses a second portion, the host is likely to be hurt or insulted or feel like a failure. It is common for dinner guests to purposely overeat, or even to eat foods they detest, in order not to offend their hosts.

Eating and cultural traditions

Food has become an essential element of nearly every kind of social gathering. It is difficult to imagine going to a party where there is no food or drink. At such events, eating is rarely a means to satisfy hunger but is instead part of the ritual, or the accepted customs of how to behave. Nowhere is ritualistic eating more evident than at celebrations. Food, usually large amounts of it, is prominent at the gatherings that follow weddings, anniversaries, school graduations, baby showers, housewarmings, baptisms, and dozens of other events. Food is also part of the ritual of mourning. Family members or friends of the deceased usually serve food to the mourners after a wake or funeral.

There are also social occasions at which food

This family is enjoying a special celebration. Eating special foods is a part of many traditional festivities.

is unquestionably the main attraction. Each of these events features specific kinds of foods that people expect to find when they arrive. The traditional food at picnics, for example, includes hot dogs, potato salad, fried chicken, and corn on the cob. At barbecues, people often eat steaks and hamburgers. At banquets and feasts, many different kinds of foods, often unusual or exotic dishes, can be found. Participants look forward to such specialties as huge sides of beef, whole stuffed pigs, and elaborate desserts. And certain holidays have become associated primarily with food. For instance, in the United States, many families stuff themselves with turkey, cranberries, and yams on Thanksgiving Day.

Food is an important factor in the traditions of

all religions. Christians, Jews, Muslims, Buddhists, and many others have special feast days. Christians, for example, traditionally celebrate Easter and Christmas with family get-togethers built around special dinners of traditional ham, turkey, or goose. "In addition," writer Rachel Epstein points out, "food plays a symbolic role in religious rituals. Christians eat wafers and drink wine during church services to re-create the sacrifice of Christ; Jews eat matzo [unleavened bread] during Passover to remember their ancestors' heroic journey from Egypt to Israel; and Muslims refrain from eating before sundown during the month of Ramadan to commemorate the first revelation of their holy book, the Koran."

A priest administers a communion wafer to a member of his congregation. Food and eating play an important part in religious rituals in every culture.

Eating anywhere and everywhere

In developed countries like the United States, Canada, and many European nations, people constantly find themselves the targets of persuasive food advertising. Food production, processing, packaging, and distribution are all huge industries. They profit each time an individual purchases a food item, so they spend a lot of money on advertising. Many television, magazine, and billboard ads emphasize the most appetizing aspects of food—appearance, aroma, and taste. Billboards and magazine ads use glossy, lifelike photos that make the viewer's appetite stir. Television commercials show actors who cannot tell the difference between a new canned spaghetti sauce and the heavenly sauce grandma used to slave over for hours.

Other ads show how foods can improve a person's image. Milk commercials, for example, show a gawky young boy or girl growing up to be a handsome young man or a beautiful young woman, thanks to the benefits of milk.

Food advertising also emphasizes food conve-

A host of fast-food establishments display eye-catching signs along a commercial street. Food advertising is a big business.

nience. Foods that require little or no preparation, that are easy to eat, and that are reasonably inexpensive enjoy widespread popularity in all developed countries. Millions of homes have microwave ovens that can cook an entire family meal in only a few minutes. After a hard day at school or work, some people who feel too tired to cook turn to quick and easy TV dinners and snack foods.

Often, people also look for speed and convenience when dining out. The fast-food industry, including such well-known restaurant chains as McDonald's, Burger King, Taco Bell, and Kentucky Fried Chicken, made more than fifty billion dollars in 1990. Also popular are pizza parlors, Chinese restaurants, and sandwich shops that deliver meals, allowing people to dine out at home. Fast food, candy, and snack foods are regular features at movie theaters, sporting events, and concerts.

In fact, because food is so plentiful and convenient in the United States, Americans tend to eat anywhere and everywhere. They eat "in the classroom; in theaters, libraries, and museums; on the street; at their desks; on the phone; in hot tubs; in cars while driving. To put it bluntly," said Joan Jacobs Brumberg, "we are indiscriminate [not very choosy] about where we eat."

Food is an accepted and important element of home life, social occasions, religious holidays, entertainment and sports events, advertising, big business, and public activity. With such widespread pressure to eat, it is not surprising that many people are tempted to eat when they should not. For people with eating disorders, each day brings a new struggle to cope with food. This substance they need to survive relentlessly threatens their happiness, their health, and even their lives.

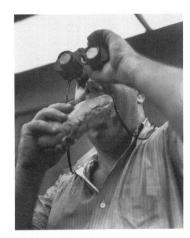

A baseball fan munches a hot dog as he follows the action on the field. Many people associate certain foods with particular events.

2

Harmful Eating Disorders

THE MOST COMMON eating disorders are compulsive overeating, bulimia, and anorexia. Compulsive overeaters and bulimics eat huge amounts of food in a single sitting, and bulimics immediately get rid of the food by vomiting or other means, such as using laxatives. Anorexics, on the other hand, eat so little that they become dangerously thin. Tens of millions of people in the United States and other countries suffer from these problems. Each disorder has certain symptoms, or characteristic signs and patterns of behavior that distinguish it from the others. Yet they are all closely related. They are parts of the same, general pattern of harmful, disordered eating. According to eating disorder specialists, most of those who develop serious eating disorders begin by following this general pattern.

Behaviors leading to eating disorders

Nearly all compulsive overeaters, anorexics, and bulimics start out trying to deal with being fat. They tend to eat too many fattening foods or to eat too much in general. As a result, they are overweight or afraid of becoming overweight. They are disappointed and unhappy with their

(opposite page) A young girl and her friend await the outcome of her weigh-in for a school health program. Since weight problems often begin at an early age, many schools try to teach students to become more conscious of what they eat.

23

physical appearance; they have what doctors call "poor body image." Their desperate attempts to change that image lead them to diets and other methods of weight loss. As these attempts repeatedly fail, they resort to more extreme methods of controlling their weight. Eventually, they develop one or more eating disorders, which means that their eating and dieting habits are out of control. Because virtually all eating problems and disorders are directly connected to the process of overeating and gaining excess weight, people

Walter Hudson tells reporters in his Hempstead, New York, living room how he reduced his weight from 1,200 pounds to 825 pounds in three months. For sixteen years, extreme obesity had prevented Hudson from walking from his bedroom to his living room.

with different eating disorders often exhibit some of the same behaviors.

Fear of having a fat body is something all people with eating disorders have in common. At one time or another, most people who tend to overeat fear that they might become obese. Obesity is a condition characterized by an excessive amount of adipose, or fatty, tissue. Although definitions for obesity vary among medical authorities, most doctors agree that a person who is more than 20 percent above ideal weight is obese. A person's ideal, or natural, weight is the weight doctors have concluded is the healthiest, considering such factors as height, body frame, and age.

Although obesity is not an eating disorder, the fear of becoming obese is a major factor in the development of these disorders. This fear leads many people to begin dieting. Medical experts estimate that more than eighty million people in the United States alone are on some kind of diet. This is what supports the American diet industry, which makes twenty billion dollars a year. All this dieting may have a number of different outcomes. For example, the person dieting may succeed in losing the desired amount of weight. But less than 2 percent of overweight people who diet actually manage to reach their goal and keep the weight off. It is more likely that the person will lose a few pounds, then go off the diet and gain the weight back.

Many Americans are overweight. This is often due to a diet high in fats and sugars and a lack of physical exercise.

An increased desire for food

As a result, most people who diet become habitual dieters, constantly gaining and losing weight. And habitual dieting is unhealthy because it can lead to an increased desire for food. Many dieters find that the more they deny themselves food, the more obsessed they become with the idea of eating. Eventually, they give in to the urge

Sue Peel and her son Jeff, of Cincinnati, Ohio, display the pants they used to wear before they each lost more than a hundred pounds on a reducing program.

to eat whatever they want. When this happens, they may binge, or consume a very large amount of food at one time. They hope that further dieting will offset an occasional "harmless" episode of splurging. But this pattern of behavior is far from harmless. It is a symptom of an eating disorder called compulsive overeating. A compulsion is an irresistible urge to do something. In this case, there is an overwhelming urge to eat.

Compulsive overeating

Medical authorities argued for several years about whether frequent binge eating, or compulsive overeating, should be classified as an eating disorder. There is still a lot of disagreement among doctors about what should be considered an eating disorder, and the definitions for these disorders are constantly changing. This is because the serious study of eating disorders is so new. Widespread recognition and treatment of these problems did not begin until the 1970s. At first, doctors described binge eating merely as a symptom of anorexia and bulimia, since all bulimics and many anorexics engage in binging. Since the late 1980s, however, most eating disorder experts have recognized compulsive overeating as a separate disorder.

Compulsive overeaters typically binge at least twice a week for several months or more. During binges, they usually consume large quantities of sweets and highly caloric foods, such as ice cream, cake, cookies, doughnuts, and potato chips. They may also eat cereal, hamburgers, or anything else that appeals to them. The amount of food eaten during binges can be enormous: a gal-

High-calorie, low-nutrition snack foods are often favored by binge eaters.

lon of ice cream, an entire cake, or two boxes of cereal with cream. Some binge eaters report consuming as many as twenty thousand calories in a single sitting, the amount an average person eats in eight days.

After a few months of binging, compulsive overeaters often stop binging for a few weeks or months and go on a diet in an attempt to lose whatever weight they gained. After some or all of the weight is lost, they begin binging again. Compulsive overeaters usually experience repeated weight changes of ten to twenty pounds or more. There are also sufferers who binge several times a week, or even several times a day. Some of these people may eventually give up on dieting and become obese.

Why compulsive overeating is harmful

Compulsive overeating is physically harmful because the repeated weight gain and loss it causes interfere with the body's metabolism. This is the series of processes by which the body con-

A microscopic view of human fat cells. The body stores excess energy from food in the form of fat and burns stored fat for energy during times of low food intake.

verts food into energy. When a person eats, the body uses digestive juices and other chemicals to break down the food into its basic components, including the nutrients essential to maintaining life. The nutrients move through the bloodstream to the cells. Chemical reactions in the cells then burn the nutrients, converting them into energy. This energy keeps the body moving and operating properly.

Much of the energy produced by the cells is in the form of heat. That is why the inside of the body is so warm. To determine the amount of heat produced in the body by food, scientists use a unit of measurement called a calorie. Foods are said to "contain" calories, which means that there is a certain amount of potential energy stored in them. A food that contains one hundred calories, such as a potato of average size, will produce one hundred calories of energy in the form of heat when burned by the body.

The body stores excess nutrients, those it does not need right away, as fat. That is why a person who eats more food than his or her body burns gains weight. Foods that contain many calories are referred to as fattening. The fat-storage process also works in reverse. If the amount of food eaten is less than the body needs, the body begins to burn the calories stored in the fat. As the fat disappears, the person loses weight.

Metabolism changes

When a compulsive overeater alternately binges and diets, his or her weight goes up and down. The metabolism constantly tries to adjust to this changing situation. The body tries to burn calories at an even rate, but as each new diet starts, the number of calories available to the body decreases, and the metabolism slows down a little to compensate. A slower metabolism does not burn calories and eliminate fat as quickly as before. So the more the weight goes up and down, the more the metabolism is thrown off—and the harder it becomes to lose weight.

Binging in secrecy

Compulsive overeating can also be mentally and emotionally harmful because of the way it dominates and disrupts a person's life. Almost all compulsive overeaters binge in secrecy. They often plan ahead for their binges, scheduling them for times when they will be alone. They are usually ashamed of their behavior and do not want others to know about it. They are aware they have a serious problem because once they get the urge to binge, they cannot stop themselves from eating. They have no control. After binging, they are often depressed and disgusted with themselves. Their excess weight and inability to deal normally with food make them very unhappy.

Consider the case of Gwen, reported by eating disorder expert Donald A. Williamson:

> ⊼ Gwen was a 33-year-old mother of three children. . . . During her 20s, Gwen [gained 40 pounds and] went on several crash diets involving very restrictive eating. She would . . . inevitably break the dieting by eating snacks, especially sweets or cereals. After violating her dietary rules, she would usually think, "Well, I might as well go ahead and eat." This . . . inevitably led to binges which were done in complete secrecy [followed by depression]. Typical binges included eating several boxes of cookies or cereal, ice cream, and/or candy. She was careful to hide the boxes or wrappers so that her husband could not see them. . . . Gradually, over the next eight years, she became more obsessed with binging. . . . Her . . . depression continued to worsen. . . . Recently, she had begun to awaken during the night and found that she could return to sleep only after eating.

No one knows how many people, like Gwen,

suffer from the harmful effects of compulsive overeating. Few studies have been done, and most of these were conducted on college campuses. Rough estimates for the number of habitual binge eaters on these campuses range from 10 to 40 percent of student populations. If the percentage is the same in the general population, there are millions of compulsive overeaters in the United States alone.

Like Gwen, most compulsive overeaters try to control their weight with episodes of dieting. This usually fails, and they remain overweight. For some, the thought of being fat is so intolerable that they resort to more extreme methods of weight control. They may then become anorexic or bulimic.

Almost all anorexics, like people with other eating problems, begin by having trouble with excess weight. Some may gain only a few pounds. Others actually become obese. Either way, they have an intense fear of becoming or remaining fat, and they react by dieting. Unlike compulsive

This woman was the first person officially diagnosed with anorexia. She was literally starving herself out of fear of being fat.

overeaters, however, anorexics diet so severely that they literally starve themselves. Most anorexics consume only about two hundred to five hundred calories a day, perhaps one-fifth or less of the amount eaten by an average person. Because they eat so little, they lose a great deal of weight. But although they reject food, they still strongly desire it, and many anorexics occasionally binge. They may eat large amounts of highly caloric foods, such as ice cream, cookies, or sour cream. Like compulsive over-eaters, they hope to prevent any weight gain from their binges by continued dieting.

Anorexics are obsessed with thinness. No matter how thin they get, they still think they are overweight. Ellen Erlanger explains in her book on eating disorders that anorexics suffer from "distorted body image," a more extreme form of poor body image. This "means that anorexics view their bodies very differently than other people do. When they look in the mirror, they never see themselves as being too thin. They 'feel fat,'" Erlanger says. For this reason, anorexics do not believe that their constant refusal to eat is a problem.

The goal is thinness

In their pursuit of thinness, anorexics often use other methods of weight loss along with severe dieting. They might perform overly strenuous exercises in an attempt to burn off extra calories. They use diet pills to curb their hunger. They also use laxatives, medications that stimulate bowel movements, and diuretics, or water pills that stimulate urination. In addition, anorexics sometimes resort to vomiting as a way of feeling thinner or eliminating calories. But whatever the method, the primary goal is thinness.

Most anorexics encountered by doctors are girls and young women between the ages of

Exercise, touted as an effective method of weight reduction, can, like food, become an obsession.

twelve and twenty-two. Older women and men also suffer from anorexia, although in much smaller numbers. Studies conducted in the United States, Great Britain, and Sweden suggest that about 1 percent of young women in developed, affluent countries suffer from anorexia. That means that in an average high school of two thousand students, of which half are girls, at least ten may be suffering from anorexia.

Why anorexia is harmful

Anorexic behavior is extremely harmful, both physically and mentally. As anorexics eat less and less, their bodies burn and use more and more of their fatty tissues. Eventually, nearly all of their fatty tissues will disappear. But the body still requires nutrients in order to continue functioning. So muscle tissues are burned and depleted, and an anorexic's weight may eventually drop to seventy pounds or less.

Because they do not eat enough, anorexics suffer from malnutrition, a lack of proper nutrients, including proteins and vitamins. This condition, usually seen only in poor, starving populations, causes many physical problems. Among these are thinning hair, low body temperature, low blood pressure, and dry skin. Anorexics also often have trouble sleeping. They run a high risk of sudden death from heart failure because their bodies are burning muscle tissue in order to survive. Since the heart is a muscle, its tissues are also used up, making it weaker.

In addition, the everyday life of an anorexic is severely disrupted by the illness. Although they frequently deny having a problem, nearly all anorexics feel nervous, guilty, and depressed. Some resort to suicide. Medical authorities estimate that 15 to 20 percent of those who suffer from anorexia eventually die from malnutrition, heart failure, suicide, or other causes related to their disorder.

The typical anorexic, then, progresses from overeating and weight gain to dieting, often to binge eating, and finally to starvation. There are a few exceptions to this pattern. Donald Williamson points out that "some anorexics do not report gaining weight or being overweight prior to the development of anorexia. These cases are a clear minority, however." Most anorexics, he says, are like Lynn, who was

> an 18-year-old high school senior. She was an excellent student, usually making all A's. . . . Lynn had been a popular child throughout childhood, but was somewhat shy. Also, she had always been a little overweight, something which her parents had often criticized. Her problems related to anorexia can be traced back to about age 14. At this time, she was approximately 15 pounds overweight at about 130 pounds. She began dieting with some of her friends and took up jogging as a form of exercise. . . . She was able to lose 15 pounds in about two months by eating only once per day and jogging from 2 to 5 miles per day. She was very pleased with herself and received many compliments from friends, family, and teachers. Once she tried to begin eating normally, she immediately gained a few pounds, which was very distressing. She again resumed restrictive eating habits . . . [which] became more and more rigid over time. . . . She tried to eat no more than two meals per day, but found that she was obsessed with eating and binged frequently. This binging frightened her very much and she usually responded by exercising vigorously. Also, she occasionally used laxatives after binging, taking two or three at a time. By the time she was 17, she had found that it was easier to control her weight by simply not eating. . . . She rapidly lost weight . . . to below 105 pounds and her parents contacted the family doctor.

The doctor diagnosed Lynn as anorexic and tried to help her but she continued refusing to eat. Her

Healthy eating habits include the ability to choose healthy foods and avoid eating empty calories.

grades went down, and she suffered from depression. After another year, she had to enter a hospital for treatment.

Anorexia is not the only extreme method of controlling weight. While anorexics attempt to avoid weight gain by rejecting food, bulimics allow themselves to go ahead and eat. But they try to stay slim by getting rid of the food immediately after it is eaten, before it can be absorbed by the body.

Bulimia nervosa

Bulimics begin as compulsive overeaters. They binge uncontrollably on large quantities of food on a regular basis. But, unlike compulsive overeaters, who either try to diet or just accept being overweight, bulimics purge, or get rid of, the food they eat. Most often, purging consists of vomiting up the food just eaten. Bulimics also use laxatives and diuretics to rid themselves of food. They engage in a regular routine of binging and purging, which usually occurs at least two or three times a week. Some bulimics binge and purge as often as several times a day. Almost always, bulimics are secretive about this behavior.

Until the 1970s, doctors thought that bulimic behavior was a symptom of or an odd form of anorexia. This seemed logical. Bulimics and anorexics both try to avoid weight gain by extreme methods. Many anorexics binge and most occasionally use purging methods. For a while, doctors used terms like "bulimic anorexics" and "bulimarexics" to describe people who exhibited bulimic behavior.

A separate disorder

It was not until 1980 that doctors recognized bulimia as a separate eating disorder. Medical authorities finally concluded that although the two disorders are obviously closely related, there are also important differences. For one thing, all bulimics binge and purge on a regular basis, while many anorexics do not. Second, bulimics usually try to maintain their normal weight, while anorexics seek to become as thin as possible. And, very important, bulimics generally recognize that they have a serious problem, while most anorexics refuse to believe they are ill.

Yet, despite these differences, the underlying similarities between the two disorders remain. They are both strong, negative reactions to excess weight gain. This helps to explain why some bulimics and anorexics periodically alternate between the two behaviors. They may starve themselves for a year or more and then suddenly start consuming enormous amounts of food and purging it.

As with the other eating disorders, it is difficult

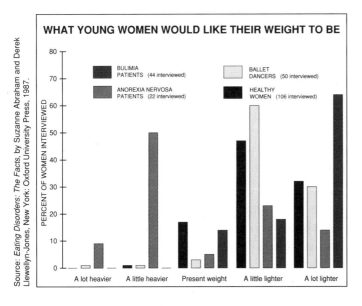

WHAT YOUNG WOMEN WOULD LIKE THEIR WEIGHT TO BE

to tell how many people suffer from bulimia. This is partly due to the lack of large-scale studies and surveys of bulimia that have been conducted. It is also due to the nature of the problem itself. Unlike anorexics, who usually lose so much weight that their problem becomes obvious, bulimics usually look normal. Because they know their eating behavior is out of control and they are ashamed of it, most bulimics do not admit their problem to others. As a result, the number of bulimics is probably much higher than the number of cases reported. There is certainly no doubt that bulimia is much more widespread than anorexia. A 1981 study found that 19 percent of the college-aged women surveyed were bulimic. Some medical authorities believe that 10 to 20 percent of the general female population may be bulimic. As with anorexia, fewer men than women suffer from bulimia. This may be due in part to the fact that society places less pressure on men than on women to be thin.

Bulimia has several harmful physical side effects. For one thing, when bulimics throw up, stomach acids come up with the vomit. Over the course of weeks and months, these acids can cause a sore throat, eat away at the enamel of the teeth, and make the mouth and jaw swell. Also, constant vomiting puts a great deal of stress on the stomach, often resulting in severe abdominal pains.

Emotional side effects

Bulimia also has emotional side effects. Bulimics commonly feel guilty and depressed about their behavior, which includes lying to conceal the disorder. Because this depression can sometimes be severe, bulimics suffer from a high rate of suicide. The misery and unhappiness that bulimia can bring to a person's life is dramatically revealed in the following personal account of Ann N:

> When I was about fourteen, food became the most important thing in my life. I found that I loved eating more than just about anything else and I started eating a lot. But then I started to gain weight . . . and I hated that as much as I loved food. . . . Then, some girlfriends told me about what seemed at the time like something too good to be true. They said if I forced myself to throw up after I ate, I wouldn't gain any weight. . . . I started eating huge amounts of food and then vomiting. I ate a dozen hard boiled eggs at a time. After I threw them up, I'd gorge myself on two or three bags of cookies . . . and so it went. At first, I had to stick my fingers down my throat in order to vomit. But after a while, I was able to bring up the food just by leaning over the toilet and opening my mouth. . . . I did all this in secret of course. I lived in terror that my parents and brother would find out. I constantly lied about what I was doing. When I was sixteen, I started getting really bad stomach cramps and sore throats. I had trouble getting to sleep at night. By then, I knew what I was doing was self-destructive, but I couldn't seem to stop myself. I wanted to ask my parents

for help but was afraid they'd completely freak out. So I got very depressed. I couldn't concentrate on anything and I started getting bad grades at school. . . . Eventually, I couldn't face it any more. When I was seventeen, I tried slitting my wrists. It didn't work but that's when everybody found out.

It has been shown that these harmful eating disorders—compulsive overeating, anorexia, and bulimia—do not occur suddenly in seemingly normal eaters. These disorders appear mainly in people who already have problems with overeating and weight gain and who have trouble coping with weight changes. A progression of increasingly desperate attempts to cope finally ends with the development of one or more of the disorders. The eating disorders are part of a larger pattern of disordered eating that has become widespread in modern, affluent societies. Doctors have just begun to understand the causes for these serious eating problems.

3

Causes of Eating Disorders

BECAUSE THE SCIENTIFIC study of eating disorders is so new, there is still a great deal of debate among experts about the causes. Doctors regularly suggest new theories about how various factors contribute to the development of eating disorders. These theories are based on information collected during extensive interviews with patients. Several patients might report that they had a similar experience or problem at a certain time in their life. For instance, they might have been criticized for being overweight as a child. Or they may have had upsetting family problems. If a doctor sees that the same experience is common among many patients, he or she might conclude that the experience is a factor that contributes to the development of eating disorders. Other doctors might disagree.

What doctors do agree about is that there is no single or primary cause of eating disorders. There are instead many factors that may combine to cause problems. Of course, no two cases are exactly alike. Individual experiences and circumstances as well as age, gender, and personality vary from one person to another. And people react differently to the same situation. How a per-

(opposite page) A girl in a scene from a television movie about anorexia refuses food even after being hospitalized for malnutrition. Despite emaciating themselves by fasting, anorexics often still "feel" fat.

41

son handles new experiences and problems can be another factor that leads to eating disorders.

Still, doctors have determined that people with eating disorders do have many things in common. Almost always, their problems began with failed attempts to control or deal with weight gain. For this reason, most doctors believe that there are some underlying causes that are common to the three disorders. These general causes may be the reason that some people have trouble with overeating and weight gain in the first place. Doctors also think that there are other factors that may cause a particular disorder to develop. These specific causes may be why each disorder is characterized by a distinct behavior.

Personal, home, and school pressures

Many people who abuse food say they do so because they are depressed. Depression is a mental state in which a person feels unusually sad and gloomy. The person may feel that a certain situation is hopeless or overwhelming or that life is meaningless. Nearly everyone feels depressed at some time, but for most people, this is a temporary feeling. For some people it is a much more serious and lasting condition. It is this more serious condition that leads to eating, and other, disorders.

There are many causes of depression. Some of them are physical and involve chemical changes in the body. Depression is also caused by emotional changes. Sad or tragic events, feelings of rejection and loneliness, or being ashamed of doing something wrong can result in depression.

Whatever the reasons for depression, sufferers often turn to food, hoping it will make them feel better. Tony B., a compulsive overeater who is also obese, said, "Every time I got depressed I ate, even when I wasn't hungry. It took my mind

Depression and other emotional problems are often the cause of eating disorders. Because eating is associated with pleasure, it temporarily diverts a person's attention from unpleasant emotions.

Source: Reprinted by permission of Bert Dodson.

off my problems and I felt like there was something good out there—food. . . . The more I ate, the better I felt."

Feelings of inadequacy

Another factor that may lead some people to eat more than they should is poor self-image. Some people see themselves as ugly, worthless, inept, or untalented. These people may feel inadequate and believe that everything difficult or unfortunate in life is a punishment for that inadequacy. Mary R. was overweight for two years and then became anorexic. When she was heavy, she often thought, "I make a mess of everything else I do. I might as well go ahead and eat and get fat. I love to eat. At least there'll be something for me to enjoy."

The feeling of inadequacy might also come from social pressures that force certain people to act in certain ways. Susie Orbach, author of *Fat Is a Feminist Issue*, says that women are at particular risk of developing eating disorders because of society's expectations. For example, women have long been raised to hide unpleasant emotions: "Nice girls don't get angry," she says. Women are taught that their role is to nurture and please others. When they have "bad" feelings, they feel guilty. Orbach states, "The roots of compulsive eating in women stem from women's position in society—she feeds everyone else, but her needs are [considered unimportant]. Food, therefore, can become a way to try to give to herself. Her fatness can become a way to express a protest at the definitions of her social role."

Many students take part in activities in which a slim figure is important. Such activities, coupled with an adolescent's desire to be attractive and popular, can pressure teens into unhealthy eating habits that may lead to eating disorders.

Parental pressures may cause eating problems in some people. For example, Terri, a young woman who binges and purges, believes her parents helped cause her problem. She says that she was somewhat overweight as a teenager but dealt reasonably well with food. However, she recalls, "My parents began to constantly badger me about losing weight. I went on diets but they never seemed to work. Each time, I gained back even more weight than before." Her frustrating pattern of alternate dieting and gaining weight eventually led her to a more extreme method of weight control—bulimia. Dietitian and eating disorder counselor Patricia Stein remembered another case involving food and misguided parents:

> Fourteen-year-old Karen realized she was the despair of her parents because she was heavy. Her mother brought her to me for assistance in losing weight. Karen told me that her mother wanted her to go on a 330-calorie-a-day formula diet [the equivalent of one average cheeseburger], even though I had tried to convey to Karen and her mother the dangers and futility of putting Karen on a strict diet. The father, in a joint session with the mother and me, maintained that he "couldn't stand fat people."

Sometimes, school pressures can influence the eating habits of young people. Often young women fear they will be criticized or left out of group activities if they are not as thin as the girls they socialize with at school. They may also fear that being overweight will keep them from being asked out on dates. These fears may push them into adopting harmful dieting patterns. At school, both male and female students feel pressure from teachers and parents to get good grades, and these expectations often cause feelings of anxiety and depression. These feelings may, in turn, lead to overeating.

Ellen Erlanger points out that, in addition,

Dancers and other performers need strong, graceful bodies. Such a need, however, can lead to an obsession with eating, dieting, or exercising in the pursuit of slimness.

many people in high school and college are involved in activities with a strong focus on weight control. If they try to diet too often or eat the wrong foods, they may begin to abuse food. "Dancers, wrestlers, gymnasts . . . cheerleaders, distance runners, and others whose bodies are constantly on display are at greater risk. Of course, other factors help determine whether eating disorders develop or not. But people whose activities provide a built-in preoccupation with weight need to be especially cautious," Erlanger says. Patricia Stein describes a young woman she counseled named Debbie. She was benched from her school drill team because she was 1.5 pounds overweight. This followed a complaint by a school official that "cows" should not be allowed on the team. Debbie was so upset that she was ready to fast for days in order to lose the weight. Luckily, her mother and Stein talked her out of it.

Conscious of weight

Debbie's situation is just one example of the tremendous emphasis modern society places on being slim. "We are very weight conscious," Erlanger says, "and the value we place on thinness has grown in recent decades. We admire people who are trim and we look down on people who are overweight. For example, the average weight of Miss America Pageant contestants and winners has gone down every year for the last twenty years." The situation was different a few decades ago, Stein points out. Most people did not worry about weighing too much or going on a diet. "The more popular young women," she says, "were usually plump and curvaceous [shapely]. In the 1950s and early '60s, a comparatively fat (by today's standards) Marilyn Monroe was promoted as having the ideal female body. Then, along came Twiggy, an anorexic-appearing model, who became the . . . feminine ideal." While many of today's models are once again showing curves, Marilyn Monroe's softness has been replaced with athletic firmness, and slim remains the ideal.

The shift in attitudes

Stein and others primarily blame the media, advertisers, and clothes designers and manufactures for the shift in attitudes. The argument is that these groups are largely responsible for creating the trend toward thinness. Stein claims, "One has only to open the morning newspaper, read a women's magazine, or watch television to become instantly aware of the thinness of advertising models and movie and television stars today, as well as of aggressively merchandised [advertised] weight-reduction programs and products. It is no secret that tremendous media pressure is placed on women of all ages to be slim and therefore, it is implied, more desirable."

In fact, selling weight-reduction programs has become an industry worth twenty billion dollars a year in the United States. Magazines and tabloid newspapers regularly include articles describing "new" or "foolproof" diet plans. Blurry "before" pictures of fat, unhappy-looking people contrast with bright studio portraits of happy, slender "afters." Television commercials with the exciting feeling of music videos show slim superstars, such as the singer Cher, sweating, working out, and promoting the benefits of health clubs and diet plans. Most of these advertisements and commercials state or imply that overweight people are unattractive.

In the 1960s, fashion model Twiggy set a new standard of thinness for women that is still felt in the 1990s.

Attitudes form early

Attitudes about thinness and fatness form early in life. Usually, children pick up ideas about what body types are acceptable or unacceptable from

A billboard advertises a diet product. People are barraged by thousands of similar messages exalting a slim figure as the key to happiness.

parents, friends, and television programs. Ellen Erlanger tells how preschoolers, when given a choice between thin or chubby dolls, tend to choose the thin ones. "By the second grade," she says, "youngsters describe overweight classmates as 'lazy' and 'stupid,' even though these labels are inaccurate and unfair."

"Children are not alone in their prejudice," says Sara Gilbert, a psychologist who has worked with overweight and obese people. She cites studies that show that "people are less likely to comply with a request from an obese person than from a thin person." Another study suggests that very overweight people have less chance of being accepted at some colleges. Also, many people are turned down for employment because they are fat. Overweight people are usually seen as "having no willpower," says Gilbert. "Obese people are seen by others, including the obese themselves, as less worthy of respect than are other people."

Eating-disorder researchers believe that society's emphasis on thinness can be harmful for some people. Fear of obesity and the desire to be thin and acceptable are powerful motivations for overweight people to diet. Most do so without the supervision of a doctor or dietitian. They often starve themselves unnecessarily and then begin abusing food. Eventually, they develop eating disorders. Even those who are only moderately overweight often feel compelled to put themselves on overly strict diets, say the researchers.

There is little doubt that the pressures to be slim are unusually strong on women. "From adolescence onward," Gilbert explains, "females are more greatly affected than males by the climate of prejudice against fatness. . . . In this climate it is thought by many people that large numbers of women are more . . . [likely] than ever before to . . . [develop] eating disorders, in particular anorexia nervosa and bulimia."

Anorexic development

Once they have begun habitually overeating and dieting, some people run the risk of developing an eating disorder. But why do some food abusers become anorexics, while others become compulsive overeaters or bulimics?

Doctors suggest that anorexics tend to focus on certain issues more than other people do. In dealing with issues such as dependence on others, anorexics express themselves through starvation. "The person may be trying to break out of her dependence on others," Ellen Erlanger explains. "If she has been strongly protected or overshadowed, she may be seeking some way to fight back or take a stand. She does not feel comfortable asserting herself in more normal ways." Jean J., an anorexic who was eventually hospitalized at a weight of eighty-two pounds, described her starving as her way of taking charge of her life. "All the important decisions in my life were made by other people . . . my parents, teachers, etc.," she said. "But I decided what went into my own mouth. When it came to my body, I was in charge." Sara Gilbert says, "The ability to diet and stay thin becomes an outward sign to the rest of the world that the woman is in control."

Extremely high standards

Anorexics also use food to express their perfectionism, the tendency to set extremely high standards for oneself or others. Anorexics are often high achievers who strive to get good grades, keep well-ordered rooms, and please other people. Many researchers believe that dieting and the elimination of excess weight become part of the anorexic's overall effort to achieve perfection. Some doctors think this drive to achieve begins as a way to please parents. The parents may have very high expectations for their child, or show affection only when the child accomplishes some difficult goal. "I was a good girl," recalls Karen D., a former anorexic. "I got all A's at school and always became friends with my teachers. . . . At home I did at least half the housework without even being asked and kept my room immaculate [extremely clean]. . . . But no matter how hard I tried, it was still difficult to get praise from my parents. It was like they just expected me to be perfect. . . . I think my anorexia was a way to show them that I could have a perfect body too. Of course, I know now how distorted my images of myself were. My emaciated [very thin] body was anything but perfect."

Confusion about feelings of sexuality and growing up is common for preteen and teenage

Anxieties about their attractiveness to others can lead teenagers to develop eating disorders in an attempt to cope with a poor body-image.

girls. Some are uncomfortable with their maturing bodies. They realize that they will soon have to deal with boys and dating and begin acting like adults. Most young women outgrow their confusion and feelings of awkwardness. But some do not. Anorexics, in particular, may cling to the "shelter of childhood," according to Erlanger. The thinner they get, the less their hips and breasts show. Also, anorexia often causes menstruation to stop. According to this view, the anorexic tries, in a sense, to return to the comfort and simplicity of childhood.

Body weight is as much a concern for compulsive overeaters and bulimics as it is for anorexics. Sara Gilbert says, "The one consistent major finding of all studies of bulimics [and compulsive overeaters] is that most of them feel fat all of the time, and most have an ideal desired weight of at

School pressures may influence the eating habits of young people. Sometimes, feelings of inadequacy lead to harmful eating patterns.

least 10 percent below their current weight. . . . Such is their concern that some may weigh themselves several times a day, while others . . . avoid the scales for fear of what they might see." Like anorexics, bulimics and compulsive overeaters are dissatisfied with their body image. But unlike anorexics, they have a less distorted view of what they look like. They know what their ideal weight is and strive to reach it without resorting to starvation. Thus, they may use less severe dieting and, in the case of bulimics, purging to achieve their goal.

Compulsive overeaters neither purge their food nor starve themselves. Why is it that some binge

Eating disorders are often a desperate attempt to cope with or to avoid the uncertainties and responsibilities of life.

eaters begin purging or starving, while others never cross over the line into bulimia and anorexia? Some doctors say that this is partly due to the degree of desperation involved. Some binge eaters are not as upset about being overweight as others are. Their weight may change frequently, but they may feel that they can deal with these changes. Many compulsive overeaters believe that they can eventually overcome their binging habits without professional assistance. In reality, this is rarely the case. Also, most say they are repulsed by the thought of vomiting up their food or starving themselves. Alan, who was a compulsive overeater for more than ten years, recalls:

> I knew about people with anorexia and bulimia but I never thought of myself as being remotely like them. Throwing up all the time . . . turning yourself into a walking skeleton? I saw all that as pretty disgusting. I figured, "These are sick characters. Me? I just like to eat. Sure, I get these urges to go out and overdo it with junk food, but so what? I eat plenty of good food too. And I keep in shape. Sure, I need to lose a few pounds, and eventually I will." You see? I didn't really realize that I had a serious problem. Each time I binged, I told myself it would be the last time. . . . I was sure I could control it if I really put my mind to it. Only later, after I got some help, did I realize that I had some of the same problems as the people I called sick characters.

Many compulsive overeaters and bulimics say that a stress of some kind usually triggers their binging or binging and purging behavior. "For about 40 percent of bulimics," Gilbert explains, "the onset of binge eating is associated with lifestyle changes or with difficulty experienced with particular emotions such as depression, loneliness or boredom." The same is true of compulsive overeaters. By contrast, anorexics rarely turn toward food when they are under stress. The reasons they deal with stress differently are still unknown.

Acquiring good eating, work, and grooming habits pays off in increased self-confidence and healthy self-esteem.

Many eating-disorder researchers say there is also an important physical cause of binge eating. It is called food deprivation. This is the result of denying oneself food by dieting. A number of studies indicate "that the experience of deprivation itself nurtures [creates] the desire to binge eat," Gilbert says. Put in a simple way, when a person goes on a diet, the body thinks it is starving and tries to get its owner to eat by enhancing the appetite. Eventually, the person may binge and begin an endless cycle of dieting and binging. Jane Hirschmann, an eating-problems counselor, explains:

> The restraints of a diet [can] lead to a binge, regardless of the personality, character, or starting weight of the dieter. Through years of clinical practice, we have concluded that dieters are like

tightly wound springs—the more restrained their dieting, the tighter the spring. Once a dieter goes off his or her diet, the spring releases. The tighter that spring has been wound, the more forceful is its release. The more restrictive the diet, the bigger the binge. . . . The compulsive eater consents to deprive himself of food—to diet—but he inevitably "cheats." He calls it cheating because he fails to see that breaking the diet is his [body's] attempt to preserve [food] supplies. . . . As we see it, the fight to hold on to something important—food—is at the heart of the diet/binge cycle. Diets create rather than cure compulsive eating.

In fact, the widespread practice of food deprivation through dieting may be one of the major underlying causes of all eating problems. Sara Gilbert says, "Obese people, slim people on diets . . . [binge eaters], and anorexics all have in common the experience of long periods of deprivation and if indeed deprivation itself is a causative factor, then this would explain the similarities across the . . . groups."

Doctors and medical researchers hope that continued studies of eating problems and disorders will lead to a better understanding of their causes. In particular, they want to find out why some factors, such as stress, depression, and food deprivation, are involved in so many eating problems. These same factors seem to lead some people to become obese, others to become compulsive overeaters and bulimics, and still others to become anorexic. Doctors realize that the more they know about the causes of food abuse, the more effective the treatments of these disorders will become.

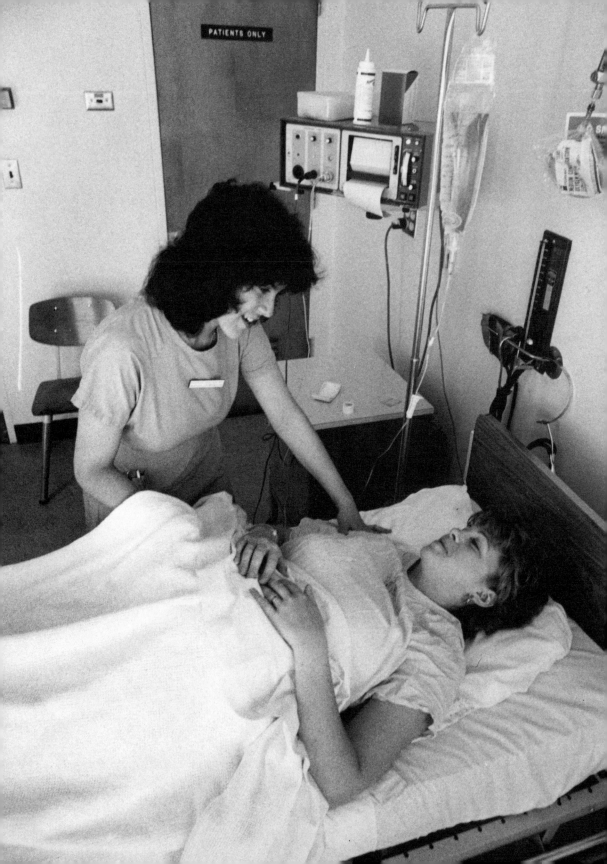

4

Treatment of Eating Disorders

TREATING EATING DISORDERS is most often a very difficult process. There are three important reasons for this. First, doctors still do not fully understand the causes of these disorders. Second, the effectiveness of any treatment is affected by the individual personality and background of the patient, how much the patient cooperates in the treatment, the amount of support given by the patient's family and friends, the particular method of treatment chosen, and the sensitivity of the doctor. The third reason is the importance of food. It is essential to life. Food abusers cannot begin their treatment by eliminating the object of their obsession. They must instead learn to deal with food in a healthy manner, and this can be very difficult.

Existing treatments for eating disorders are either physical treatments of the body or psychological treatments, in which the doctor tries to shape the patient's emotions and behavior. Sometimes, psychological methods alone will help a patient. In other cases, doctors use both physical and psychological methods. They know that every case is different and that the same method or combination of methods that helps one patient

(opposite page) People with severe eating disorders are sometimes hospitalized for treatment.

57

Group counseling is effective in helping persons with eating disorders modify their behavior. Members share stories and problems associated with their disorders and gain support from each other in their struggle to regain control of their lives.

may not help another.

The most common form of physical treatment for eating disorders is providing the patient with needed food and care through hospitalization. Most often, this method is used in severe cases of anorexia. As Ellen Erlanger explains, when "medical and counseling professionals feel that a person's life and/or stability is in danger, hospitalization is necessary. The top priority is keeping the person alive." The length of the hospital stay varies according to the seriousness of the case. The patient may stay for as little as a few weeks or as long as two months or more.

The first and most important part of the treatment is to make the patient gain some weight. This is almost always difficult at first, because most anorexics continue to deny their problem and refuse to eat. Sometimes, the patient eats a normal meal in order to please parents, doctors, and nurses. But after they leave the room, he or she runs to the bathroom and vomits. Therefore, it is often necessary to have someone in the room at all times to monitor the patient. In a few cases, feeding tubes have to be used. Usually, doctors try to get the patient to take in three thousand to five thousand calories per day, perhaps six to ten times what he or she is used to consuming. This can result in a weight gain of up to fourteen pounds in a month.

Making decisions

During the hospital stay, doctors begin talking to the patient about the problem. The primary goal here is to convince the person that he or she is indeed sick. The patient is told that his or her cooperation in the treatment is essential to recovery. Eventually, through skilled care, a feeling of trust may be built between the patient and the medical staff. When this happens, the doctors may allow the patient to make some of his or her own decisions about the kind and amount of food eaten. When the patient is strong enough and convinced that there is a real problem, psychological treatment begins.

Another physical treatment for anorexia is drug therapy. During the 1960s and 1970s, doctors experimented with various drugs they hoped would remove patients' fear of eating. One of these substances was chlorpromazine, which some doctors reported helped in a number of cases. However, this drug has several negative side effects, such as lowering blood pressure and reducing body temperature. It is only occasionally used today.

An alternative approach in drug treatment of anorexia is the use of antidepressant drugs. By affecting certain chemicals in the brain, antidepressants reduce or eliminate a patient's state of depression, which appears to be an important cause of anorexia in a majority of cases. There is con-

Depression often causes eating disorders. Antidepressant drugs sometimes help depressed persons regain emotional balance and enable them to control their eating problems.

siderable disagreement among doctors about the usefulness of antidepressants in treating anorexia. Some claim a moderate rate of success, while others say they have not found the drugs to be particularly effective. There is increasing interest among doctors, however, in the use of antidepressants to treat bulimia. Many bulimics treated with these drugs have shown a reduced tendency to binge and purge. Apparently, eliminating depression in bulimics helps them abandon their destructive eating habits. But drug therapy alone is not the cure, and it is always accompanied by psychological treatment.

Psychological approaches

Doctors sometimes use a psychological method called behavior modification to treat eating disorders. This is a step-by-step process that attempts to modify, or change, a patient's eating behavior. The doctor and patient decide together on a list of goals to be achieved. For an anorexic, these might include eating all the food on the plate during each meal or gaining a certain amount of weight each week. For a bulimic, the goals might be to refrain from vomiting after eating or to substitute several nutritious meals for one unhealthy binge. For binge eaters in general, small changes in eating behavior are encouraged,

An anorexic young woman weighs herself. Anorexic and bulimic persons' obsession with their weight can often be treated with psychotherapy.

such as eating slower, drinking water before meals, or leaving food on the plate.

Then, these positive behaviors are reinforced. Each time the patient achieves a specific goal, he or she is given a reward. Usually, the reward takes the form of a privilege. For example, the patient might be allowed to participate in certain social activities, receive more visitors, or use the telephone more often.

Of course, for this procedure to work, the patient must be closely controlled and monitored. For this reason, some doctors, including Hilde Bruch, have been critical of behavior modification. They say the method is not effective in the long run because patients cannot be controlled and monitored forever. Once on their own, the

The most common psychological treatment for eating disorders is counseling therapy.

patients often slip back into harmful eating behaviors.

Supporters of behavior modification say that some patients are able to monitor themselves. One way they do this is to keep a food diary, a daily log that records the amount of food eaten, the circumstances, and the patient's feelings before and after eating. The patient shows the diary to the doctor every few weeks and together they evaluate the progress made. Like other methods of treatment, behavior modification appears to be effective in some cases and ineffective in others.

Recovery through counseling

The most common psychological treatment for eating disorders is psychotherapy, or counseling therapy. The goal of this method is to help the patient understand the causes of the problem and learn to deal with these causes. The doctor begins by explaining to the patient exactly why the particular eating behavior is harmful. Together, the doctor and patient attempt to identify what factors in the patient's life contribute to the behavior. They discuss the patient's life-style, fears and concerns about food and eating, and causes of related problems, such as stress and depression. During repeated counseling sessions, the doctor tries to help the patient cope with stress, improve body image, and establish more normal eating patterns.

Counseling therapy takes a number of different forms. The initial meetings between doctor and patient are called one-to-one sessions. Many doctors recommend that patients eventually move on to group therapy. In these sessions, four, five, or more people suffering from the same disorder meet and share their experiences and concerns. The doctor leads the discussion, offering emotional support and factual information when appropriate.

Doctors have found group therapy to be espe-

A physician discusses food-related health problems with an overweight girl.

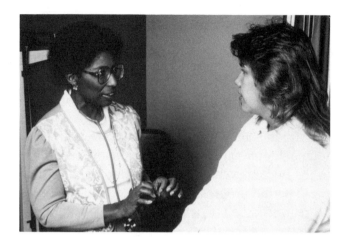

cially effective for compulsive overeaters and bulimics. Many of these people are unaware that their eating problems are so common. Some see themselves as misfits, different from and inferior to "normal" people. This makes them feel worthless and ashamed. In group sessions, they discover that they are not alone, that many seemingly average people have gone through the same ordeal. They draw strength and emotional support from each other. Jerry R., a former bulimic, recalls:

> My experiences with the group made a huge difference. At first, I didn't say much. . . . I was afraid of what the others would think. But then, I heard them tell how they did the same things I did. Finally, I opened up. . . . I let it all pour out. I remember that I cried and two of the others held me and said they knew how I felt. I felt I wasn't alone anymore. I think we all felt like we had some strength to give each other, even when we didn't have any for ourselves.

Another form of counseling therapy for eating disorders involves sessions in which the family or spouse of the patient participates. According to Ellen Erlanger, this approach "may be used when the therapist feels that family issues and attitudes have contributed to the disorder, or that the family's strengths can be used to help solve underlying problems. The therapist will observe the family's communication patterns, roles, and values and give recommendations for ways to improve communication. Such help can be especially helpful to adolescent clients and their families, or to couples whose relationships are . . . undergoing severe strain."

Other kinds of help

Local support groups for people with eating disorders can be found in many cities and towns in the United States. Like the people who take part in group therapy, members of support groups

A teen volunteer staffs a hotline as part of a teens-helping-teens support program in Boston, Massachusetts.

meet periodically to share stories and information. Most often, a recovered food abuser or a family member of an anorexic or bulimic leads the meeting. Support groups offer surroundings in which people with eating problems can feel comfortable and speak freely about their worries and experiences. In a way, a support group picks up where group therapy leaves off, allowing the members to continue strengthening one another. Sometimes, a member may be having emotional or other problems and fear falling back into a harmful eating behavior. He or she can phone or meet with another member of the group, usually even on short notice or at odd hours. They talk about the problems and try to find other solutions besides abusing food.

An important first step

Self-help organizations are support groups that reach out to people on a statewide or national level. Self-help groups offer an important first step for people who know they have an eating problem and are looking for help. These organizations publicly advertise their addresses and phone numbers. Anyone can call them and ask for advice or information about various food problems. Most of the groups will also suggest hospitals, doctors, or local support groups that may be of assistance to the caller. Although the caller is talking to a stranger, staff members are usually people who used to have eating disorders themselves, so they are understanding and sensitive to the caller's problems. Some of these organizations are listed in the back of this book.

Proper nutritional advice can also be an important aid in recovering from eating disorders. Efforts to overcome poor eating habits, improve distorted body image, and eliminate starvation or binging patterns may be hindered if the person is not eating the right foods. Often, it is not the amount of food but the type of food eaten that can cause problems. For instance, a recovering binge eater may decide to stay away from high-carbohydrate foods, such as sweets, breads, grains, and starches—the foods most often eaten on prior binges. But the body needs a certain amount of carbohydrates daily in order to satisfy energy needs. Eliminating these foods entirely only creates a state of carbohydrate deprivation that increases the desire to binge. A dietitian or doctor can provide information about which foods are best and how a balanced diet makes abusing food less likely.

The goal of every eating-disorder treatment is the same. That goal is to help patients learn to deal with food in a normal, healthy way. Recovery means achieving ordered rather than disordered eating habits.

5

An Approach to Ordered Eating

THIS CHAPTER IS not aimed at people who have serious eating disorders like anorexia or bulimia. Nor is it aimed at people who are obese. Those who suffer from these problems need to see a doctor who specializes in eating problems. For these sufferers, concerns with eating habits and body weight have become the primary issues in life. A competent professional can show them how to sort out and deal with their feelings and return to healthy eating habits.

The purpose of this chapter is to help healthy eaters remain that way. This does not mean that following the advice given here will guarantee that they will never acquire an eating disorder. As shown earlier, many factors, some of them involving feelings and emotions, can cause these problems to develop. But often, eating problems begin with poor eating habits. The habits lead to weight gain, which, in turn, can lead to depression and food abuse. Following is a simple guide to healthy eating habits, based on sound advice from doctors and dietitians.

It is natural for people to be concerned about their weight. Society equates slimness with beauty and success, so many people worry about

(opposite page) A young woman includes a variety of nutritious foods in the balanced meal she is preparing.

Debra Sue Maffett won the 1983 Miss America beauty pageant. Many Americans believe that Miss America is the ideal of feminine beauty, an ideal many women find impossible to achieve.

the amount of food they eat. There is a widespread belief that people who eat a lot automatically get fat. This is not always the case. The simple fact is that some people can eat more than others. Everyone is born with a different ability to burn calories and, therefore, a different capacity for food. Some people burn calories very quickly and do not easily gain weight. These are the people whose friends often say jokingly, "I hate you because you can eat like a horse and still stay thin." Other people burn calories more slowly and gain weight easily.

Those who have a tendency to gain weight often think they are overweight when they are not.

They tend to judge themselves by the artificial ideals of slimness established in the media, in magazines, and in movies. Their weight and shape may not conform to these ideals, but that does not necessarily mean that they are overweight. It may just mean that the weight and shape natural and suitable for them are different from what appears in the popular culture. But many people refuse to accept this idea. They believe they can force their bodies to conform to society's ideals by eating less food. They may go on strict diets, and this is where many eating problems begin.

Reducing diets

Most people should avoid going on reducing diets, except when advised to do so and supervised by their doctor. A reducing diet is one in which someone consumes less than his or her daily calorie requirement, the amount of food needed to maintain a natural, ideal weight. Daily calorie requirements can be found in the tables in the calorie-counter booklets available at supermarket checkouts. The figures in these tables are general ones. A person's actual calorie requirement may be a bit lower or higher than the figure listed.

Nature did not intend for people to eat less than their daily calorie requirements. The fact that 98 percent of reducing diets ultimately fail proves that the human body is not designed for such dieting. When people do eat less than nature intended, their bodies fight back. As explained earlier, reducing diets create a state of food deprivation that often leads to a cycle of dieting and binging. It is far more healthy for a person to eat a normal amount of food and to learn to accept his or her natural weight.

But what about the people who already weigh

This chart shows the total number of calories that the average person should eat each day.

RECOMMENDED CALORIE ALLOWANCES		
	Age Group	**Calories**
Children:	1–3	1,300
	3–6	1,600
	6-9	2,100
Boys:	9-12	2,400
	12-15	3,000
	15-18	3,400
Girls:	9-12	2,200
	12-15	2,500
	15-18	2,300
Men:	18-35	2,900
	35-55	2,600
	55-75	2,200
Women:	18-35	2,100
	35-55	1,900
	55-75	1,600

Source: Encyclopedia Americana

more than what is natural, or ideal, for them? What about those who are 5 to 20 percent, or moderately, overweight? If they do not go on a reducing diet, how can they ever hope to return to their ideal weight? The answer is to go on an "eat right" rather than an "eat less" diet. This means regularly eating their daily calorie requirement and making sure they get a proper nutritional balance. This does *not* mean counting and worrying about the number of calories consumed. The body instinctively knows how much food it needs and signals that need by creating a feeling of hunger. Simply eating when hungry and stopping when the feeling of hunger is gone will ensure the appropriate calorie intake.

People who are moderately overweight and follow a proper eating plan will eventually reach their ideal weight. But it will take time. Weight loss will be very slow as the body readjusts to a healthy state. These people may lose only a pound every two weeks, or even a pound every month. The important thing is that they will get used to eating in a healthy manner and be less likely to gain the weight back. And they will not feel deprived of food, so their chances of developing harmful eating patterns and disorders will be reduced.

Developing healthy eating habits is not only a matter of eating the right amount of food. The

Dietary experts have revised the traditional four food groups to reflect modern concerns about weight and a healthy cardiovascular system. Choosing foods from these groups will best maintain health, these experts claim.

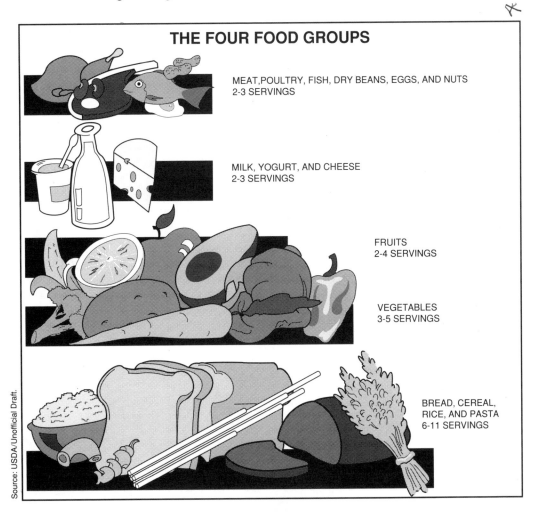

THE FOUR FOOD GROUPS

MEAT, POULTRY, FISH, DRY BEANS, EGGS, AND NUTS
2-3 SERVINGS

MILK, YOGURT, AND CHEESE
2-3 SERVINGS

FRUITS
2-4 SERVINGS

VEGETABLES
3-5 SERVINGS

BREAD, CEREAL, RICE, AND PASTA
6-11 SERVINGS

Source: USDA/Unofficial Draft.

way people eat and the kind of food they eat are also important. Often, these factors are as much a part of gaining excess weight as eating too much.

Thinking about eating habits

Most people do not think about the way they eat until they are noticeably overweight or have a serious eating problem. They do not realize that when and how they eat affect the way the body deals with food. Often, they develop bad eating habits without realizing it. For instance, they may eat even when they are not hungry because of social pressures or other reasons. A good rule of healthy eating is never to eat when not hungry. On the other hand, one should never be afraid to eat when he or she *is* hungry. As mentioned earlier, many people feel they must deny themselves food in order to lose weight. Hunger is the body's

way of saying it needs fuel, and the healthiest thing to do is to fuel up and avoid food deprivation. In fact, it is best not to go too long without eating. The longer a person remains hungry, the more deprivation one feels and the more likely it is the person will compensate by overeating later.

Custom and tradition

Some eating habits are reinforced by custom and tradition. For example, most people eat three meals a day. They do not question whether this is the best way to eat. They just do it because it is what everyone else does. Eating three major meals a day is certainly not unhealthy. Eating five or six smaller meals, however, over the course of the day is better for the body for two reasons. First, the body more easily digests and breaks down a small amount of food than it does a large amount. It actually burns more calories and stores fewer calories as fat when it deals with small, regular quantities of food. Second, eating smaller, more frequent meals regularly satisfies hunger and reduces periods of food deprivation. Eating this way makes the urge to overeat less likely.

The physical acts of eating, chewing, and swallowing can also affect the amount of food eaten. Most compulsive overeaters and bulimics say that they eat very quickly, take large bites, chew very little, and often take a second bite before they have swallowed the first. Although they may not realize it, they actually taste very little of what they eat. This means their appetite is not satisfied and they want to eat more. It is better to eat at a slow pace, take small bites, chew food thoroughly, and swallow one bite before taking another.

Also, many doctors recommend drinking a glass of water before or during every meal in addition to the drink that goes with the meal. For

Regular, moderate exercise combined with a healthy diet can maintain fitness and ideal weight.

one thing, water increases the feeling of fullness, which helps keep a person from eating too much. The water also helps in digestion and keeps food moving through the body at a steady rate.

People's eating habits are influenced by the amount of exercise they get. People who get very little exercise do not burn as many calories. Their bodies may store more calories as fat, resulting in excess weight gain. Regular, moderate exercise helps the body burn the right amount of calories and maintain a healthy combination of muscle and fat.

As mentioned earlier, eating habits are also influenced by emotions. Eating to relieve stress, anxiety, depression, loneliness, or boredom can only lead to harmful eating patterns. People who find themselves eating for any of these reasons should seek help from a counselor or doctor. There is no need to be ashamed. Everyone experiences one or more of these emotional problems from time to time. It is better to eliminate the problem early before it develops into a much bigger problem such as an eating disorder.

Knowing what to eat

It does little good to eat the right amount of food in the right way if the food is the wrong kind. Most people know very little about nutrition. They tend to believe the statements made in food advertising or the advice of friends and relatives about what is best to eat. This can lead to trouble because food advertisers often exaggerate or mislead, and friends and relatives may know much less than they think they do. As a result, many people do not always get the nutrients they require.

To maintain healthy functioning, the body needs certain kinds of nutrients every day. The three basic nutrients are proteins, carbohydrates, and fats. Proteins are the building blocks the body uses to make skin, muscle tissue, and other body parts. The body uses fats as a source of energy and vitamins. Carbohydrates are also an important energy source and provide many essential vitamins and minerals. The body works best when it gets these three nutrients in the correct proportions. According to dietary experts, the healthiest diet contains about 15 percent protein, 35 percent fat, and 50 percent carbohydrates.

Proteins are found in meats, fish, and other seafoods, and dairy products like milk, cheese, and yogurt. Plants contain proteins, too, although

Vegetable and animal sources can provide dietary protein. Experts have determined that a variety of sources is most healthful.

in smaller amounts. This explains why people who eat vegetarian diets can be perfectly healthy. People have many wrong ideas about how much protein to eat. As Edward Edelson, science editor of the *New York Daily News*, points out, "Several decades ago, the prevailing belief was that a lot of protein was better than a little. That belief has changed now, for science has shown that Americans eat too much protein." An average American man needs only two or three ounces of protein each day to maintain health. A nine-ounce piece of chicken or three pints of milk will provide that amount. But most Americans consume two, three, or four times that much protein each day. One problem is that a person who eats too much protein may not be getting the right proportions of other nutrients.

Fats also come from animal products such as meat and milk, as well as from plants. Some fats are less healthy than others. Fats that come from red meat and dairy products are called high-density, or saturated, fats. Those from plants and white meats like chicken and fish are called low-density, or less-saturated, fats. The body has a much harder time digesting and efficiently using all of the elements in saturated fats, which contribute to heart disease and other problems. Therefore, it is healthier to get into the habit of eating more foods that contain less-saturated fats and fewer foods with saturated fats.

Carbohydrates are made up of sugars. Some are simple sugars, like the ones found in candy bars, frostings, and honey. These contain little or no nutritional value. Other sugars are more complex, so they are referred to as complex carbohydrates, or starches. These are vital to the body because they contain many important vitamins, minerals, and other essential substances. Grains, breads, pasta, beans, and potatoes are rich in complex carbohydrates.

Ignorance about carbohydrates often leads to problems with weight gain. Many people still ac-

Dairy products, a rich source of protein, can also contain high levels of saturated fats.

Many people eat candy and other sugary snacks for an energy boost. The body can only use so much sugar at one time, however; the rest is converted to fat. Eating complex carbohydrates, like grains, can reduce sugar cravings.

cept the misconception that eating too many starches is fattening and unhealthy. For this reason, they may consume much less than their 50 percent daily requirement of carbohydrates. This causes deprivation and a strong craving for carbohydrates. Unfortunately, many people feed that craving by eating candy, cake, and other sweets that contain mainly nonnutritious, simple carbohydrates. These foods also contain a lot of saturated fat. The result is often weight gain and the beginning of an unhealthy cycle of dieting and overeating. It is better to eat plenty of potatoes and other low-calorie, nutritious starches in the first place. This reduces the occurrence of carbohydrate cravings.

For more information about eating a healthy

diet, it is best to consult a doctor. He or she will recommend a good book on the subject or recommend a dietitian. Getting the *right* information and putting it to work can build a lifetime of healthy eating habits.

How to Recognize Eating Disorders

FOLLOWING ARE some of the more common warning signs of eating disorders, compiled by Ellen Erlanger and other eating-disorder experts. If two or more of these feelings and behaviors happen consistently in your everyday life, you may have an eating disorder. You should see your doctor as soon as possible. If it turns out that you are indeed suffering from an eating disorder, he or she will help you understand the problem better. The doctor may begin treatment or refer you to a specialist who is more familiar with eating problems.

If you notice some of the warning signs in a friend or relative, talk to him or her about it in a friendly but honest manner. Offer some literature on the subject and suggest that he or she visit a doctor. The most important thing to remember is that people with eating disorders are not bad, weak, undisciplined, or crazy. They are average people who, for various reasons, have lost their ability to deal with food in a healthy way.

A person may be anorexic if he or she:

1. Undergoes an unusually large weight loss in a brief amount of time.

2. Constantly denies being hungry and claims to be "full" after taking only a few bites.

3. Drastically changes eating habits, eating much less than before, especially foods high in calories. Exercises for long periods, pushing hard even when very tired.

4. Appears to be afraid of gaining weight.

5. Displays strange patterns of handling food—for

instance, pushing it back and forth on the plate but not eating it. Develops a strong interest in cooking but refuses to eat the food he or she prepares.

6. Experiences a disruption or complete loss of menstruation.

7. Undergoes changes in personality and behavior, such as becoming nervous or depressed or wanting to be alone often.

A person may be a compulsive overeater if he or she:

1. Is of fairly normal body weight but is constantly concerned about being fat.

2. Consistently attempts to control body weight by dieting.

3. Frequently alternates between binging and dieting.

4. Displays secretive behavior, especially about food.

5. Is depressed and ashamed after binging.

6. Eats large amounts of high-calorie foods on binges.

7. Often leaves behind or tries to conceal containers and wrappers from high-calorie or junk foods.

A person may be bulimic if he or she shows the above signs of compulsive overeating and/or:

1. Consistently attempts to control body weight by vomiting and/or laxative and diuretic abuse.

2. Appears to engage in a cycle of binging and purging.

3. Frequently uses the bathroom to vomit.

Glossary

---

adipose tissue: Fatty tissue.

anorexia nervosa: An eating disorder characterized by self-starvation.

antidepressant: A drug that reduces or eliminates a state of depression.

appetite: The desire, or craving, for food, often a specific kind of food.

behavior modification: A step-by-step therapy that attempts to change a patient's habits by controlling his or her actions and giving rewards to reinforce positive patterns.

binge: To eat an unusually large quantity of food—most often high-calorie, fatty, easily digested food—at one time.

bulimia nervosa: An eating disorder characterized by repeated binging and purging.

calorie: A unit of measure of heat energy.

compulsive overeating: An eating disorder characterized by repeated binging and dieting.

counseling therapy, or psychotherapy: Treatment in which a doctor and patient discuss the causes of the patient's problem and plan ways to overcome it.

depression: A mental state characterized by deep sadness and unhappiness.

diuretic: Medication that stimulates urination.

food deprivation: The denial of food to the body, which causes cravings and other physical reactions.

laxative: Medication that stimulates bowel movements.

menstruation, or period: A normal physical process that occurs about every twenty-eight days in women, in which blood and cell debris are discharged from the uterus.

perfectionism: The tendency to set extremely high standards for oneself or others.

purging: The voluntary act of vomiting after eating.

Organizations to Contact

The following organizations are concerned with the issues covered in this book. All of them have publications or information available for interested readers.

American Anorexia/Bulimia Association (AA/BA)
133 Cedar Lane
Teaneck, NJ 07666
(201) 836-1800

AA/BA acts as an information and referral service. It offers counseling, collects information on eating disorders, and organizes self-help groups. It also maintains a speakers bureau of people qualified to lecture on the subject of eating disorders.

Anorexia Nervosa and Related Eating Disorders (ANRED)
PO Box 5102
Eugene, OR 97405
(503) 344-1144

ANRED collects and gives out information on eating disorders and provides support groups, medical referrals, and counseling. It also conducts workshops, conferences, and training programs to help professionals identify, understand, and treat eating disorders.

National Anorexic Aid Society (NAAS)
5796 Karl Road
Columbus, OH 43229
(614) 436-1112

NAAS provides community education programs and self-help groups for victims and their families. It compiles a state-by-state listing of doctors, hospitals, and clinics treating eating disorders. In addition, it provides parents, educators, family physicians, and clergy with information that will aid in the early recognition and treatment of these disorders.

National Association of Anorexia Nervosa and Associated Disorders (ANAD)
Box 7
Highland Park, IL 60035
(312) 831-3438

ANAD seeks a better understanding of, as well as prevention of, eating disorders. It encourages and promotes research on the causes and treatments of these disorders and also acts as a resource center, compiling and providing information. ANAD fights against the production, marketing, and distribution of dangerous diet aids and the use of misleading advertisements. It also cosponsors meetings, conducts surveys, and provides a speakers bureau and children's services.

Suggestions for Further Reading

Jane Brody, *Jane Brody's Nutrition Book.* New York: Bantam Books, 1977.

Joan Jacobs Brumberg, *Fasting Girls: The History of Anorexia Nervosa.* New York: New American Library, 1988.

Ellen Erlanger, *Eating Disorders.* Minneapolis: Lerner Publications, 1988.

Jane R. Hirschmann and Carol H. Munter, *Overcoming Overeating.* New York: Fawcett Columbine, 1988.

Sheila MacLeod, *The Art of Starvation: A Story of Anorexia and Survival.* New York: Schocken Books, 1982.

Lisa Messinger, *Biting the Hand That Feeds Me: Days of Binging, Purging, and Recovery.* Novato, CA: Arena Press, 1986.

Cherry Boone O'Neill, *Dear Cherry: Questions and Answers on Eating Disorders.* New York: Continuum Publishing, 1985.

Cherry Boone O'Neill, *Starving for Attention.* New York: Dell, 1982.

Geneen Roth, *Breaking Free from Compulsive Eating.* New York: Macmillan, 1984.

Terence J. Sandbek, *The Deadly Diet: Recovering from Anorexia and Bulimia.* Oakland, CA: New Harbinger Publications, 1986.

Ronald F. Schmid, *Traditional Foods Are Your Best Medicine.* Stratford, CT: Ocean View Publications, 1987.

Michele Siegel, Judith Brisman, and Margot Weinshel,

Surviving an Eating Disorder: New Perspectives and Strategies for Family and Friends. New York: Harper & Row, 1988.

Donald A. Williamson, *Assessment of Eating Disorders: Obesity, Anorexia, and Bulimia Nervosa.* New York: Pergamon Press, 1990.

C. Philip Wilson, ed., *Fear of Being Fat: The Treatment of Anorexia and Bulimia.* New York: Jason Aronson, 1985.

G.T. Wilson and L. Lindholm, "Bulimia Nervosa and Depression," *International Journal of Eating Disorders,* Vol. 6, 1987.

Works Consulted

W.S. Agras, *Eating Disorders: Management of Obesity, Bulimia, and Anorexia Nervosa.* New York: Pergamon Press, 1987.

American Psychiatric Association, *Diagnostic and Statistical Manual of Mental Disorders.* Washington, DC: American Psychiatric Association, 1980. Rev. ed., 1987.

Hilde Bruch, *Conversations with Anorexics.* New York: Basic Books, 1988.

Hilde Bruch, *Eating Disorders: Obesity, Anorexia Nervosa, and the Person Within.* New York: Basic Books, 1979.

Graham D. Burrows et al., eds., *Handbook of Eating Disorders: Obesity.* New York: Elsevier Science Publishers, 1988.

Peter Dally and Joan Gomez, *Obesity and Anorexia Nervosa: A Question of Shape.* London: Faber & Faber, 1980.

E.G. Duchmann and D.A. Williamson, "Bulimia, Dietary Restraint, and Concern for Dieting," *Journal of Psychopathology and Behavioral Assessment,* Vol. 11 (1989).

Sara Gilbert, *Pathology of Eating.* New York: Routledge & Kegan Paul, 1986.

James E. Mitchell, *Anorexia Nervosa and Bulimia: Diagnosis and Treatment.* Minneapolis: University of Minnesota Press, 1985.

M.S. Palazzoli, *Self Starvation.* New York: Jason Aronson, 1985.

Harrison G. Pope and James I. Hudson, *New Hope for Binge Eaters.* New York: Harper & Row, 1984.

Patricia M. Stein and Barbara C. Unell, *Anorexia Nervosa: Finding the Life Line.* Minneapolis: Compcare Publications, 1986.

Richard B. Stuart and Barbara Davis, *Slim Chance in a Fat World.* Champaign, IL: Research Press Company, 1972.

Albert J. Stunkard, *The Pain of Obesity.* Palo Alto, CA: Bull Publishing, 1976.

Jill Welbourne and Joan Purgold, *The Eating Sickness: Anorexia, Bulimia, and the Myth of Suicide by Slimming.* Brighton, England: The Harvester Press, 1984.

Index

About the Author

Don Nardo is an actor, film director, and composer as well as an award-winning writer. As an actor, he has appeared in more than fifty stage productions. He has also worked before or behind the camera in twenty films. Several of his musical compositions, including a young person's version of *The War of the Worlds* and the oratorio *Richard III*, have been played by regional orchestras. Mr. Nardo's writing credits include short stories, articles, and more than twenty books, including *Lasers: Humanity's Magic Light; Anxiety and Phobias; The Irish Potato Famine; Exercise; Gravity: The Universal Force; The Mexican-American War;* and *Medical Diagnosis.* Among his other writings are an episode of ABC's "Spenser: For Hire" and numerous screenplays. Mr. Nardo lives with his wife, Christine, on Cape Cod, Massachusetts.

Picture Credits